Cooking Around the World

Recipes From

Italy

Dana Meachen Rau

Raintree

Chicago, Illinois

Edited by Abby Colich, Laura Knowles, and
John-Paul Wilkins
Designed by Cynthia Akiyoshi
Picture research by Tracy Cummins
Production by Vicki Fitzgerald
Originated by Capstone Global Library
Printed and bound in China by Leo Paper
Products Ltd

17 16 15 14 13
10 9 8 7 6 5 4 3 2 1

**Library of Congress Cataloging-in-
Publication Data**
Rau, Dana Meachen, 1971-
 Recipes from Italy / Dana M. Rau.
  pages cm.—(Cooking around the
world)
 Includes bibliographical references and
index.
 ISBN 978-1-4109-5973-7 (hardback)
 1. Cooking, Italian—Juvenile literature. I.
Title.

TX723.R38 2014
641.5945—dc23   2013017272

Acknowledgments
The author and publisher are grateful to
the following for permission to reproduce
copyright material: Capstone Publishers
pp. 1, 9–11, 16–43 (Karon Dubke);
ChooseMyPlate.gov p. 12 (with thanks
to USDA's Center for Nutrition Policy
and Promotion); Getty Images pp. 7
(Adrian Weinbrecht), 13 (JGI/Jamie Grill),
14 (Lew Robertson), 15 (Henglein and
Steets); Shutterstock pp. 4 (Emi Cristea),
5 (Manamana), 6 (Tupungato).

Design elements reproduced with
permission of Shutterstock (Alex
Studio, Andrey Savin, Angel Simon,
anistidesign, Arkady Mazor, Brooke
Becker, Christian Jung, draconus,
Fedorov Oleksiy, giorgiomtb, IngridsI,
Luis Santos, marchello74, Mazzzur,
Nordling, oksana2010, photastic, Piccia
Neri, Picsfive, Richard Peterson, rook76,
Sandra Cunningham, Tim Ackroyd, Tobik,
ULKASTUDIO, Viktar Malyshchyts,
Volosina).

Cover photograph of a pizza margherita
reproduced with permission of Capstone
Publishers (Karon Dubke).

We would like to thank Ruth Ben-Ghiat,
Sarah Schenker, and Marla Conn for their
invaluable help in the preparation of this
book.

Every effort has been made to contact
copyright holders of any material
reproduced in this book. Any omissions will
be rectified in subsequent printings if notice
is given to the publisher.

All the Internet addresses (URLs) given in
this book were valid at the time of going
to press. However, due to the dynamic
nature of the Internet, some addresses
may have changed, or sites may have
changed or ceased to exist since publication.
While the author and publisher regret any
inconvenience this may cause readers, no
responsibility for any such changes can
be accepted by either the author or the
publisher.

Contents

Ancient and Modern

Italy is easy to find on a map. At the base of the continent of Europe, Italy looks like a boot dipping its toe into the Mediterranean Sea.

The land varies throughout the country. Skiers enjoy the mountainous Alps on the northern border. Vacationers enjoy the coast of the Italian Riviera. In the south, an active volcano, Mount Etna, looms over the island of Sicily.

The Tuscan countryside is bathed in sunshine for much of the year.

Throughout its long history, Italy has been a center of art and culture. Thousands of years ago, Rome, the current capital of Italy, ruled the Roman Empire. This empire stretched west into Europe, north into Britain, east into Asia, and south into parts of Africa. Over water and land, Rome traded new goods and traditions with its conquered regions. Rome influenced the art, science, and literature of the known world.

Today, Italy has a diverse community. The north contains more cities, while the south has more farmers. Like many modern cities around the world, Italian cities are filled with large apartment and business buildings. In older sections, however, you can still see the narrow streets and piazzas, or city squares, from long ago. In the countryside, towns and villages are filled with people who have close ties to their families and communities.

Italy is a modern country that still holds memories of its past. Children pass the ruins of the Colosseum on their way to school. Friends play soccer on a field that was once a chariot racetrack. People may take a lunch break sitting at the base of an ancient marble statue. The richness of Italy's past is still a part of Italian life today.

A network of canals weaves its way through the beautiful city of Venice. Tourists flock to the city from all over the world.

5

Buon Appetito

Pasta and pizza may be the first things to come to mind when you think of Italian food. But they are only a small part of it. Italy's many regions have developed their own special dishes. In areas near the coast, seafood is an important part of many meals. Rice grows best in the Po Basin of northern Italy. Almond trees thrive in the heat of the south. Even specific cities and towns are known for certain foods, such as prosciutto ham in Parma, grilled steak in Florence, and risotto in Milan. Northern Italian meals are known to include rice, butter, and cream. Southern Italian dishes often contain olive oil, tomato, and pasta.

Come rain or shine, Italians visit outdoor markets for a selection of fresh ingredients.

Italian Meals

An Italian's day starts out with a quick breakfast. Lunch is the largest meal. In many towns, stores and businesses close from noon until around 4:00 p.m. so that people can enjoy this meal at home. Dinner is a much lighter meal eaten later in the evening.

Food and family go hand in hand in Italy. Mealtimes are a chance to relax and enjoy some quality time together.

Traditionally, a large Italian meal has many courses. *Antipasto* means "before the meal" and often includes small pieces of cured meats and cheeses. The *primo piatto* (first course) is a small plate of pasta or risotto, or a bowl of soup. The *secondo piatto* (second course) is a meat or fish dish. Finally, *dolce* (dessert) is often fresh fruit or another sweet creation.

Before Italians begin to eat, they may wish for a good meal for everyone—*Buon appetito!*

7

Italian Ingredients

Here are some ingredients found in Italian households and in the recipes in this book. If you can't find a certain ingredient, look for similar replacements.

Olives and olive oil give many Italian dishes their distinctive flavor. Olives are preserved in brine. Olive oil comes from olives that are pressed. Extra-virgin is the best.

Balsamic vinegar is a thick, brown vinegar with a rich and slightly sweet flavor.

Cheeses are made mostly from cow's milk in the north, and goat's and sheep's milk in the south. Some common Italian cheeses include Parmigiano-Reggiano (Parmesan), mozzarella, and gorgonzola.

Cured meats are preserved, sliced, and used for antipasti (the first course) and other dishes. Recipes in this book use prosciutto, capocollo, mortadella, and pancetta (Italian bacon).

Vegetables are piled high at Italian markets. During the right season, you'll find artichokes, eggplants, mushrooms, peas, tomatoes, carrots, celery, red peppers, and zucchinis. Italians also use lots of greens, such as arugula, radicchio, and spinach. Many dishes are seasoned with onion and garlic. Some vegetables, such as artichokes, eggplants, pepperoncini, and red peppers, are marinated in oil and vinegar and kept in jars.

Fruits are often eaten as dessert in Italy. Popular fruits include blood oranges, pears, lemons, melons, plums, pomegranates, strawberries, and figs.

Herbs and spices, such as basil, parsley, thyme, sage, rosemary, hot red pepper flakes, and anise, flavor many Italian dishes.

Nuts help add texture to desserts. Commonly used nuts include almonds, pistachios, pine nuts, hazelnuts, and walnuts.

Pasta comes in hundreds of types—long strings, short tubes, and many other shapes. Many Italians make their pasta fresh, but they also use dry pasta. Many varieties of pasta, both dry and fresh, can be found in supermarkets and Italian grocery stores.

Cornmeal is used to make polenta, a dish in northern Italy that often replaces pasta or bread with a meal. It can be cooked like porridge or grilled like a patty.

Arborio rice is short-grain rice from northern Italy used to make a creamy dish called risotto.

Meat is the basis of the second course of an Italian meal. Veal, lamb, beef, pork, chicken, and rabbit are popular choices.

Beans are a source of protein for Italians. They use cannellini beans, chickpeas, and fava beans.

Seafood and shellfish are eaten fresh, such as scampi, mullet, mussels, squid, and branzino, or packed in oil, such as tuna, sardines, and anchovies.

Eggs are used for baking, but also for omelets called frittatas.

Bread and breadsticks accompany many meals to help soak up sauces or to top with treats from an antipasto platter.

Italian meals contain a delicious combination of fresh fruits, vegetables, and cheeses.

How to Use This Book

Each chapter of this book will introduce you to aspects of Italian cooking. But you don't have to read the book from beginning to end. Flip through, find what interests you, and give it a try. You may discover a recipe that becomes your new favorite meal!

Anise Cookies

Biscotti refers to all kinds of Italian cookies. These biscotti are the crunchy twice-baked kind that many Italians dip in coffee and eat for breakfast. You can dip them in milk or hot chocolate to soften them up. Anise gives them a slight licorice flavor.

Ingredients
1 cup sugar
¼ cup unsalted butter
2 eggs
¼ teaspoon anise extract
2 cups flour
1 teaspoon baking powder
¼ teaspoon salt
½ cup sliced almonds

Tools
Measuring cups and spoons
Electric hand mixer
Large and medium bowls
Spatula
Baking sheet
Parchment paper
Cooling rack
Serrated knife

If you already do a lot of cooking, you may know your way around the kitchen. But if you've never diced a tomato, sautéed garlic, or whisked up cream, don't worry. Check out the glossary on page 44.

18

Each recipe is set up the same way: Ingredients lists all the ingredients you'll be adding. Tools tells you the various kitchen utensils you will need. Collect the ingredients and tools before you start working so that you have everything nearby when you need it.

Then just follow the Steps. Be sure to read them carefully. Numbers on the photos indicate which step they refer to. Don't worry if your creation isn't perfect when you reach the end. Cooking takes practice and experimentation. Be patient and enjoy the process.

If you have to follow a specific diet, or have food allergies, look for the labels on each recipe. These will tell you if a dish is vegan, vegetarian, dairy-free, gluten-free, or if it contains nuts. However, you should check food packaging before use to be sure.

teps

. Preheat oven to 350°F.

. In a large bowl, cream together the sugar, butter, eggs, and anise extract, and beat with electric mixer until smooth.

. In a medium bowl, mix together the flour, baking powder, t, and almonds.

. Add the dry ingredients to the et ones. Stir until just combined make a soft dough. Be careful t to over mix.

. Line a baking sheet with rchment paper. Divide the ugh in half. Form each half into og about 8 inches long.

. Bake for about 30 minutes, til golden brown. Let cool about minutes on a cooling rack.

. With a serrated knife, cut each g into ½-inch thick diagonal ces. Return the cookies to the king sheet.

. Bake for about 8 to 10 minutes, til lightly toasted.

N contains uts

D airy free

G luten free

V egetarian

V egan

Quick Tip

Parchment paper makes your job easier in two ways. It keeps cookies from sticking to the baking sheet as they bake. And it makes cleanup much easier. You can find parchment paper in the baking aisle or paper product aisle of many grocery stores.

akes about 2 dozen cookies me: 20 minutes prep, 40 minutes bake

 N contains uts   **V** egetarian

VARIATION

Play around with different flavors in this breakfast cookie. Try a different kind of extract, such as vanilla or almond. Try different nuts, too, such as pistachios, walnuts, or hazelnuts.

Look at Quick Tips for cooking and kitchen advice, and Variations for swapping out ingredients for others if you would like.

Anytime you are in the kitchen, ask an adult to help or be nearby. You shouldn't use any knife or appliance without an adult's permission and assistance. Check out page 14 for even more ways to be safe while you cook.

A Healthy Kitchen

It's fun to head out on a food adventure by trying new tastes from countries beyond your own. But you should also keep your health in mind. According to ChooseMyPlate.gov, the following are the basic food groups. Italians include all of these groups in a meal, or over the course of a day, to get the proper balance of nutrients to grow and be healthy.

Fruits and Vegetables

Italians may sip a glass of blood orange juice in the mornings, or top their panna cotta with strawberries. They also include many healthy vegetables in their diets, such as spinach, peas, and red peppers. Both fruits and vegetables can help reduce your risk for certain diseases. They contain nutrients your body needs and fiber to keep your digestive system running smoothly.

Grains

These are foods made from wheat, rice, corn, oats, or other grains. Whole grains that use the entire grain kernel are the healthiest. Refined grains, such as white flour and white rice, do not have as many vitamins and minerals. Pasta, risotto, and polenta are just a few of the Italian foods in this group. Many pastas and breads come in both white and whole grain varieties.

ChooseMyPlate.gov

MyPlate shows us the importance of eating a combination of all the food groups in our diets.

Italian foods are delicious, and fun to eat, too!

Protein

Protein foods include meats, poultry, seafood, and eggs. It also includes beans (such as cannellini beans used in *pasta e fagioli*) and nuts. Look for low-fat meats. Cured meats, a favorite of Italians, have a lot of added salt. Try to eat these only occasionally.

Dairy

Cheese, ice cream, milk, and any products made of milk fall into this category. Dairy foods contain a lot of bone-building calcium. Hard cheeses, like Parmesan, soft cheeses, like ricotta, and even creamy gelato give Italians a dose of calcium. Choose low-fat options when you can.

Fats and Sugar

Some oils, especially the ones from plants, such as olive oil, do provide some important nutrients. Nuts are high in oils, too. But solid fats, such as butter and meat fat, are not as good for you. So use them sparingly. Your body needs sugar, but not too much. Try not to fill up on too many Italian sweets!

A Safe Kitchen

It can be fun to whip up a tasty new creation in the kitchen, but safety should be your number one concern. Here are some tips to keep in mind:

- Make sure an adult is nearby for permission, help, advice, and assistance.
- Wash your hands before you work.
- Wear the right clothing, including sturdy shoes and an apron.
- Foods can grow harmful bacteria. Be sure to keep foods in the refrigerator or freezer until they are ready to use. Check expiration dates. If something smells or looks funny, it may be spoiled.

It is not just the pot that gets hot when you are boiling water. Be careful of the water and steam, too.

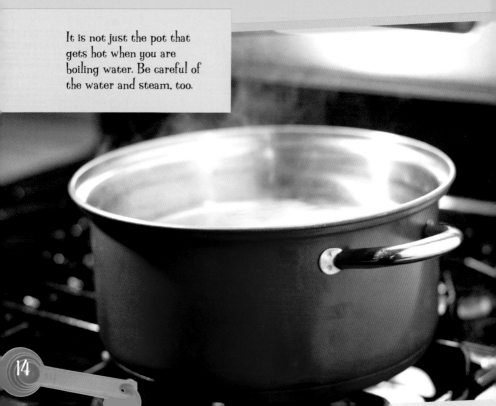

There are lots of delicious meals to try in Italian cooking. But remember to share the fun of cooking with an adult.

- Raw meat, poultry, seafood, and eggs can carry germs. Always wash your hands immediately after touching them. Wash any knife or cutting board after you use them with these foods and before you use them again. Make sure these foods are cooked all the way through before you eat them. Clean countertops and kitchen tools with warm, soapy water when you are done working.

- On the stovetop, be sure pot handles point in, so the pots don't get knocked over. Never leave pots unattended. Do not let anything flammable, such as loose sleeves or kitchen towels, near burners on the stove.

- Always use oven mitts when removing a pan from the oven or microwave. Avoid steam when you lift a top off a pot on the stove or in the oven.

- Knives are sharp. Always point the blade away from you. Take your time and pay attention to what you are cutting. Don't use a knife without the help of an adult.

Buongiorno!
(Good Morning!)

For many Italians, a good morning means starting with something sweet. People often stop into pastry shops or coffee bars on their way to work or school. They might get a drink, such as a cappuccino (a foamy mix of coffee and milk) or a glass of blood orange juice, and a pastry or cookie. They stand at the counter or sit at an outdoor table to enjoy this tasty part of their day.

Cornetti

Cornetti are the Italian version of a French croissant. These flaky pastries are shaped like small horns. They can be plain or filled with cream, fruit, nuts, or chocolate.

Ingredients

1 sheet frozen puff pastry dough, thawed

About 3 tablespoons chocolate hazelnut spread

1 egg yolk

1 teaspoon milk

Sugar for sprinkling

Tools

Rolling pin

Knife

Cutting board

Measuring spoons

Spreader

Baking sheet

Small bowl

Whisk

Pastry brush

Steps

1. Preheat oven to 425°F.

2. Unfold the puff pastry dough. Roll it with a rolling pin to flatten any seams. Cut the sheet into 4 squares, and then cut each square diagonally into 2 triangles so that you have 8 triangles in all.

3. Place about 1 teaspoon of hazelnut chocolate spread in the center of each triangle and spread it around. Be careful not to spread right to the edges. Roll up the triangles loosely from one side to the opposite point. Place them on a baking sheet.

4. In a small bowl, whisk together the egg yolk and milk. Brush onto each cornetto. Sprinkle them with sugar.

5. Bake for about 12 minutes, or until browned.

Makes 8 cornetti
Time: 15 minutes prep, 12 minutes bake

Ncontains **uts**   **V**egetarian

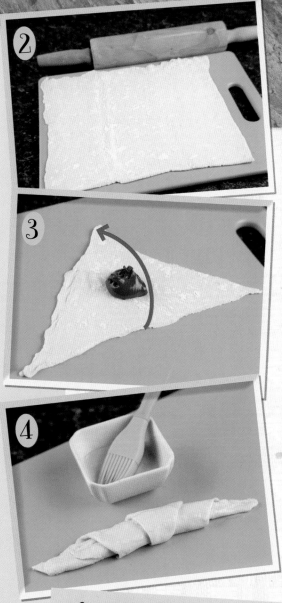

Variation

Instead of chocolate hazelnut spread, you can spread any type of fruit jam inside the cornetti, too. Or combine both chocolate hazelnut spread and jam together!

Anise Cookies

Biscotti refers to all kinds of Italian cookies. These biscotti are the crunchy twice-baked kind that many Italians dip in coffee and eat for breakfast. You can dip them in milk or hot chocolate to soften them up. Anise gives them a slight licorice flavor.

Ingredients

1 cup sugar
¼ cup unsalted butter
2 eggs
¼ teaspoon anise extract
2 cups flour
1 teaspoon baking powder
¼ teaspoon salt
½ cup sliced almonds

Tools

Measuring cups and spoons
Electric hand mixer
Large and medium bowls
Spatula
Baking sheet
Parchment paper
Cooling rack
Serrated knife

Steps

1. Preheat oven to 350°F.

2. In a large bowl, cream together the sugar, butter, eggs, and anise extract, and beat with an electric mixer until smooth.

3. In a medium bowl, mix together the flour, baking powder, salt, and almonds.

4. Add the dry ingredients to the wet ones. Stir until just combined to make a soft dough. Be careful not to over mix.

5. Line a baking sheet with parchment paper. Divide the dough in half. Form each half into a log about 8 inches long.

6. Bake for about 30 minutes, until golden brown. Let cool about 15 minutes on a cooling rack.

7. With a serrated knife, cut each log into ½-inch-thick diagonal slices. Return the cookies to the baking sheet.

8. Bake for about 8 to 10 minutes, until lightly toasted.

Makes about 2 dozen cookies
Time: 20 minutes prep,
        40 minutes bake

Nuts contains

Vegetarian

Quick Tip

Parchment paper makes your job easier in two ways. It keeps cookies from sticking to the baking sheet as they bake. And it makes cleanup much easier. You can find parchment paper in the baking aisle or paper product aisle of many grocery stores.

Variation

Play around with different flavors in this breakfast cookie. Try a different kind of extract, such as vanilla or almond. Try different nuts, too, such as pistachios, walnuts, or hazelnuts.

Fresco e Delizioso (Fresh and Delicious)

For hundreds of years in Italy, markets were one of the main places where people met, gathered, and shared news. That is still true today. Customers often shop daily, stopping at separate booths to buy cheese, meat, fruits, vegetables, and herbs. Italians keep their recipes simple to bring out the most flavor from these fresh ingredients.

Antipasti

In Italy, antipasti are served before a meal for a special occasion. This platter can be a colorful display to showcase the meats, cheeses, and marinated vegetables of Italy. Serve it with some crusty bread or grissini. Grissini are breadsticks invented in Turin in the 1600s.

Ingredients

1 bag of spring mixed greens (including arugula and radicchio)

¼ pound each prosciutto, capocolla, and mortadella

½ pound each provolone, fresh mozzarella, and Parmesan

Various jars of marinated vegetables, such as eggplant, artichoke hearts, roasted red peppers, pepperoncini, and black and green olives

Olive oil

Balsamic vinegar

Italian bread or grissini

Tools

Large platter

Knife

Cutting board

Steps

1. Cover the platter with the greens.

2. Roll the individual slices of cured meats. Cut the cheese into slices or bite-size pieces. Arrange the meat and cheese on top of the lettuce.

3. Fill in open areas with the various marinated vegetables.

4. Lightly drizzle olive oil and balsamic vinegar over the platter.

5. Serve with slices of bread or grissini.

Makes about 8 to 10 appetizer servings
Time: About 20 to 30 minutes

Panzanella Salad

This salad is a popular side dish in Tuscany, a region in the middle of Italy that includes the city of Florence. When bread sits out in the open air, it may become dry and crunchy. Instead of wasting this stale bread, Italians combine it with fresh herbs and vegetables to make a colorful salad.

Ingredients

Stale Italian bread, cut into ½-inch cubes (about 2 cups)

2 large tomatoes, chopped

1 cucumber, peeled and chopped

½ small red onion, thinly sliced

1 sprig basil, torn into small pieces

5 tablespoons olive oil

Salt and pepper, to taste

Tools

Measuring spoons

Bowls

Knife

Cutting board

Spoon

Plastic wrap

Steps

1. In a bowl, combine the tomatoes, cucumber, onion, basil, olive oil, and salt and pepper.

2. In another bowl, place about half of the bread cubes. Spoon half of the tomato mixture over the bread. Place the rest of the bread into the bowl, and spoon over the rest of the tomato mixture. By making layers, the juices will better soak into all the bread pieces.

3. Cover with plastic wrap. Let sit at room temperature (not the refrigerator) for a few hours for the flavors to blend together.

4. Stir well before serving. Add salt and pepper to taste.

Quick Tip

Don't put tomatoes in the refrigerator. They taste best when left at room temperature. In the fridge, they will turn soft and grainy and lose their fresh flavor.

Makes 4 to 6 servings
Time: About 15 minutes (plus a few hours for flavors to combine)

 Dairy free   **V**egetarian

23

Panino di Parma

A *panino* is an Italian sandwich. This panino combines the flavors of the city of Parma, home to prosciutto ham and Parmesan cheese. These ingredients, joined by arugula and balsamic vinegar, create an interesting play of sweet and salty in your mouth.

Ingredients

Focaccia bread

½ pound thinly-sliced prosciutto

2 ounces Parmesan cheese

1 large handful arugula

1 to 2 tablespoons balsamic vinegar

Tools

Knife

Cutting board

Vegetable peeler

Bowl

Measuring spoons

Salad tongs

2

3

4

Steps

1. Slice the focaccia bread open to make the top and bottom for the sandwich.

2. Lay on a few slices of prosciutto.

3. With a vegetable peeler, thinly shave pieces of cheese and place them on the prosciutto.

4. In a bowl, toss the arugula with the balsamic vinegar. Place the dressed arugula onto the sandwich.

5. Top with the other half of the focaccia and serve.

VARIATION

Focaccia is a flat Italian bread, similar to pizza crust. But any crusty Italian bread will work well for this recipe. You can buy bread as a loaf and slice it yourself. Or look for ciabatta rolls to make individual sandwiches.

Makes 4 sandwiches
Time: About 10 minutes

Pizza Margherita

Naples is considered the home of pizza. In Naples, pizza is made in traditional wood-burning ovens. One of Naples's most famous creations is Pizza Margherita. In 1889, the city welcomed Queen Margherita and her husband King Umberto I with a pizza covered with the colors of the Italian flag—red, white, and green.

Ingredients

		Tools
Refrigerated pizza dough	1 ball fresh mozzarella	Rolling pin
Flour	A few sprigs of fresh basil	Baking sheet
Olive oil		Pastry brush
1 (14.5-ounce) can diced tomatoes, drained	Salt and pepper, to taste	Knife
		Cutting board

Steps

1. Preheat oven to 425°F.

2. Sprinkle flour on your cutting board or work surface. Roll out the dough into a rectangular shape. Transfer to a baking sheet brushed with olive oil.

3. Cover the dough with the diced tomatoes. Slice the mozzarella very thin, and place all over the tomatoes. Season with salt and pepper.

4. Bake for about 10 minutes. Take out the baking sheet, and sprinkle the basil on top of the pizza. Drizzle pizza with olive oil.

5. Return the pizza to the oven and cook for another 10 to 15 minutes, until the crust is browned around the edges and the cheese is lightly browned.

Variation

Instead of canned tomatoes, you can use fresh tomatoes for this recipe, too. Slice the tomatoes very thin, and remove the seeds. This will keep the pizza from getting too soggy.

Makes 4 servings
Time: 15 minutes prep,
20 to 25 minutes bake

Vegetarian

Basta Pasta! (Enough Pasta!)

Italians eat a lot of pasta. There are countless types of pasta to choose from. Some pasta, such as ravioli or tortellini, is filled with meat or cheese. Capellini are long, thin strands, penne are pointed tubes, and farfalle are shaped like bow ties. Use a smooth, long pasta for lighter sauces. Use pasta with grooves or holes to hold chunkier sauces. And remember to say *basta* (enough) before you feel stuffed!

Gorgonzola Gnocchi

Gorgonzola is made from the milk of cows that are raised in Piedmont and Lombardy, two regions in northern Italy. The blue veins running through the cheese are actually mold, which gives the cheese a tangy flavor. Gnocchi are little dumplings made from potatoes and boiled like pasta.

Ingredients

4 ounces Gorgonzola cheese
½ cup heavy cream
½ cup skim milk
2 (1-pound) packages potato gnocchi (2 pounds total)
Fresh parsley for garnish
Salt and pepper, to taste

Tools

Measuring cups
Saucepan
Spoon
Stockpot
Colander

Steps

1. In a saucepan, bring the milk and cream to a simmer over medium heat.

2. Turn down the heat to medium-low. Add the Gorgonzola and cook for about 5 minutes, stirring frequently, until the cheese melts and the sauce thickens slightly. Season with salt and pepper.

3. Meanwhile, cook the gnocchi in the stockpot according to package directions. Drain in a colander.

4. Toss the sauce with the cooked gnocchi. Garnish with fresh parsley.

Makes 4 to 6 servings
Time: About 15 minutes

Vegetarian

VARIATION

Look for gluten-free gnocchi in specialty stores if you want to avoid wheat flour.

Pasta with Pesto

This basil-based sauce is Genoa's best-known dish. Long ago, people made pesto by mashing the ingredients together with a mortar and pestle. But it is much faster and easier with a blender. You can serve pesto as a pasta sauce, add it to soup, or even spread it on pizza or a sandwich.

Ingredients

3 cups loosely packed basil
  leaves
¼ cup pine nuts
1 large clove garlic, minced
¼ cup olive oil
Salt and pepper, to taste
¼ cup Parmesan cheese,
  grated
1 pound dry spaghetti

Tools

Measuring cups
Knife
Cutting board
Food processor or blender
Cheese grater
Bowl
Spoon
Stockpot
Colander

Steps

1. Wash and dry the basil leaves well.

2. Combine the basil, nuts, garlic, olive oil, and salt and pepper in a food processor to create a paste.

3. Transfer the paste to a bowl. Add the cheese and stir to combine.

4. Meanwhile, cook the pasta in the stockpot according to package directions. Drain in a colander.

5. Toss the pesto with the pasta and serve.

Makes 4 to 6 servings
Time: About 20 minutes prep

VARIATION

Pine nuts are actually seeds. They come from cones of a stone pine tree. But if you can't find pine nuts, you could use walnuts to make pesto as well.

Ncontains**uts**   **V**egetarian

Tagliatelle with Bolognese Sauce

Bologna is known for this long-simmering meaty sauce served over tagliatelle, long, flat ribbons of pasta, also invented in this city. Since the sauce is so hefty, it needs pasta equal to the task of holding all this weight and flavor. If you can't find tagliatelle, you could use rigatoni (a short, wide tube) or cavatappi (thick corkscrews).

Ingredients

4 ounces diced pancetta
2 tablespoons olive oil
1 small yellow onion, diced
2 stalks celery, diced
2 carrots, diced
2 cloves garlic, minced
1 pound ground beef

Salt and pepper, to taste
½ cup beef broth
1 (14.5-ounce) can diced tomatoes
Water
1 cup milk
1 pound dry pasta
Parmesan cheese

Tools

Measuring cups and spoons
Knife
Cutting board
2 stockpots
Spoon
Cheese grater

Steps

1. Place the diced pancetta in a stockpot with the olive oil. Cook for about 8 minutes on medium-high, stirring occasionally to brown all over. Add the diced onion, celery, carrots, and garlic. Cook for about 5 to 7 minutes more until the vegetables soften.

2. Add the beef and salt and pepper. Brown the beef for about 10 minutes.

3. Add the broth and diced tomatoes (with juices) to deglaze the pan. Scrape up any brown bits that have stuck to the pan as the liquids evaporate, about 2 to 3 minutes.

4. Add the milk and bring to a simmer. Turn the heat down, and let the sauce simmer, half covered, for about 2 to 4 hours, stirring occasionally. Add water (about ¼ cup at a time) as the liquids evaporate, to keep the sauce from drying out.

5. Meanwhile, cook the pasta according to package directions. Drain and return to the pot.

6. Add the sauce and toss to combine. Serve with freshly grated Parmesan cheese.

Quick Tip

Try to dice the onion, carrot, and celery into pieces all about the same size. That way they will all take about the same amount of time to cook.

Makes 6 servings
Time: 45 minutes prep,
          2 to 4 hours simmer

Quant'è buono! (How Good It Is!)

Many Italian dishes are cooked on the stove, filling the air with delicious Italian smells that invite others to the kitchen. Eating together has always been an important part of Italian culture. Family and friends enjoy each other's company while eating meals together.

Scampi

Scampi means prawns, a type of crustacean. You can also use large shrimp for this recipe. Serve this dish over cooked pasta, or just soak up the lemony juices with some crusty Italian bread.

Ingredients		Tools
1 pound uncooked large shrimp, shelled and deveined	½ cup vegetable broth	Cutting board
	1 tablespoon dried parsley	Knife
2 tablespoons olive oil	½ teaspoon red chili flakes	Measuring cups and spoons
2 tablespoons butter		Skillet
2 large cloves garlic, minced	Salt and pepper, to taste	Spoon
	1 tablespoon lemon juice	Turner

Steps

1. Heat the oil and the butter in a skillet on medium high until the butter melts. Add the garlic and cook for about 1 minute.

2. Add the shrimp, broth, parsley, red chili flakes, salt, and pepper. Sauté the shrimp for about 2 minutes on one side. Then flip them over to cook on the other side for about 1 minute more, until the shrimp is pink and cooked through, and some of the liquid has evaporated.

3. Top with the lemon juice. Serve with pasta or bread.

Quick Tip

Watch over your shrimp the whole time they cook. Shrimp cook very fast. If you cook them too long, they will have a rubbery texture.

Makes 4 servings
Time: About 10 minutes

Pasta e Fagioli

Pasta and bean soup is one of the most common Italian soups. Different households in Italy make their own versions of this dish using different beans, pastas, and herbs. It is a hearty soup that is great for a cold day.

Ingredients

4 ounces diced pancetta

2 tablespoons olive oil

1 small yellow onion, diced

2 cloves garlic, minced

1 dry bay leaf

½ teaspoon dried thyme

½ teaspoon dried rosemary

4 cups chicken broth

1 (14.5 oz) can diced tomatoes

2 cans (15.5 oz cans) cannellini beans, drained and rinsed

1 cup dried ditalini pasta

Salt and pepper, to taste

Parmesan cheese

Tools

Knife

Cutting board

Measuring spoons

Liquid measuring cups

Stockpot

Spoon

Potato masher or fork

Bowls

Grater

Steps

1. Place the diced pancetta in a stockpot with the olive oil, onion, garlic, bay leaf, thyme, and rosemary. Cook on medium to medium-high heat until the onions soften and the pancetta is browned, about 10 minutes.

2. Add the chicken broth, diced tomatoes (with the liquid), and one can of beans.

3. Mash the other can of beans with a potato masher or back of a fork, then add to the soup.

4. Cover and bring to a boil. Then turn the heat down and simmer for about 15 minutes. Add the pasta. Turn the heat up to medium and let it simmer in the soup for about 10 to 15 minutes, or until al dente.

5. Remove the bay leaf. Season with salt and pepper. Serve in bowls, with freshly grated Parmesan cheese.

Quick Tip

Dry herbs are easy to have on hand to use when you need them. But if you want to season your soup like a true Italian, you may want to use fresh herbs. You can use fresh herbs more generously than dried herbs. A general rule is to use about 3 times more of a fresh herb than a dried one.

Dairy *free*
(without the Parmesan)

Makes 6 dinner-size servings
Time: About 50 minutes

Veal Scaloppine with Lemon Sauce

Italy is known for its veal, the tender meat from calves, especially in the region of Lombardy. In Lombardy, this dish might be served with the creamy rice dish risotto. Risotto takes patience, as you slowly stir broth into Arborio rice. If you'd rather make a meal faster, you can serve it with pasta or Italian bread instead.

Ingredients

1 pound veal scaloppine cutlets
Flour
Salt and pepper, to taste
2 tablespoons olive oil
⅓ cup chicken broth
Juice of 1 lemon (about ¼ cup)
1 tablespoon butter

Tools

Measuring cups and
    spoons
Plate
Skillet
Turner
Dish and aluminum foil
Spoon

Steps

1. Sprinkle some flour on a plate, and coat each piece of veal in the flour. Season with salt and pepper.

2. Heat the olive oil in the skillet. Place the veal pieces into the pan. Do not overcrowd them.

3. Cook about 2 minutes on one side until lightly browned. Flip over and cook about 2 minutes on the other side until no longer pink. Remove from the pan and set aside in a dish covered with foil to keep warm.

4. Add the broth, lemon juice, and butter to the pan. Bring to a boil, and cook about 1 minute, stirring constantly.

5. Put each portion of veal on a plate and pour sauce over it. Serve with pasta, bread, or risotto.

VARIATIONS

Some people prefer not to eat veal. You can make this dish with chicken instead. You may be able to find chicken prepared for scaloppine. If not, place your chicken cutlets between two pieces of waxed paper and use a kitchen mallet to pound them thin.

Makes 4 servings
Time: 20 to 25 minutes

La Dolce Vita (The Sweet Life)

Living in Italy is sometimes described as "the sweet life." That might be because Italians often take the time to enjoy each moment. Strolling through city squares or sitting outside a café for a treat is a common way to spend one's time.

Most Italian meals don't include dessert—more often an Italian might just have some dried fruit, nuts, or fresh fruit. Dolci (sweets) are often served for special occasions and help Italians truly enjoy a sweet life!

Panna Cotta

Panna cotta means "cooked cream." This traditional dessert is often served with fresh fruit or a sauce on top. You can unmold it upside down onto a plate, or just eat it out of the bowl.

Ingredients

1 cup whole milk	½ cup sugar
1 tablespoon unflavored gelatin	Fresh raspberries and blueberries (or any fresh berries)
2 cups heavy cream	

Tools

2 saucepans	6 small bowls or ramekins
Spoon	Baking pan
Whisk	Warm water
Measuring cup	Plates

40

Steps

1. In a medium saucepan, combine the milk and gelatin. Warm on medium-low heat and stir until the gelatin dissolves, about 4 to 5 minutes. Remove from the heat and set aside.

2. Add the cream and the sugar to another saucepan. Bring just to a boil over medium-high heat, stirring constantly with a whisk, until the sugar is completely dissolved, about 8 to 10 minutes. Remove from the heat.

3. Pour the cream and sugar mixture into the saucepan with the milk and gelatin mixture. Stir to combine.

4. Transfer the mixture into a large measuring cup with a spout. Use the measuring cup to pour the mixture into six small bowls or ramekins.

5. Let cool to room temperature. Then place in the refrigerator for 4 to 6 hours to set.

6. To unmold the panna cotta, set the bowl in a baking pan with some warm water to help loosen it. Then turn the bowl upside down over the serving plate. Jiggle it until it falls onto the plate.

7. Serve the panna cotta with fresh berries on top.

Gluten free **V**egetarian
(with vegetarian gelatin)

Makes 6 servings
Time: 15 to 20 minutes to prep and cook,
4 to 6 hours to set

Tartufo

This ice cream "truffle" is made to look like a luxurious black mushroom grown in Umbria that is sniffed out by specially trained dogs. But this tartufo doesn't taste like a mushroom! It is coated in chocolate and has a surprise cherry in the center.

Ingredients	Tools
Chocolate ice cream	Ice cream scoop
12 maraschino cherries	Baking sheet
2 cups semisweet or dark chocolate chips	Wax paper
	Microwave-safe bowl
2 tablespoons vegetable oil	Spoons
	Cooling rack
	Muffin pan
	Cupcake liners

Steps

1. Leave the ice cream out of the freezer until slightly soft. Scoop out a ball of ice cream, and hold it in your hand. Push a cherry into the center, and reform into a ball.

2. Place the ice cream ball on a baking sheet covered with wax paper. Repeat to make 11 more chocolate balls. Work quickly, because the ice cream will melt.

3. Place the baking sheet into the freezer. Let the ice cream balls freeze solid again, around 1 hour. (You can also work in batches, making four at a time so they don't melt as you work.)

4. In a microwave-safe bowl, combine the chocolate chips and the vegetable oil. Microwave on high for 30 seconds. Stir. Microwave for another 30 seconds. Stir until the chocolate is smooth and liquid.

5. Take the ice cream balls out of the freezer. Place on a cooling rack with a piece of wax paper underneath the rack. Spoon the chocolate mixture over each ice cream ball to coat the top and sides completely.

6. Lift each ice cream ball with a spoon, and place in a cupcake liner in a muffin pan. Place back in the freezer for another hour or more until completely hardened again.

7. Serve with a few more cherries.

Makes 6 servings
Time: About 30 minutes prep,
2 hours to freeze

Gluten free   **V**egetarian

VARIATION

Any kind of ice cream works for this dessert. Use your favorite! While the melted chocolate is still soft, you can sprinkle it with chocolate chips or chocolate sprinkles.

43

Glossary

Tools

colander	round bowl-shaped tool with holes for draining foods
cutting board	flat work surface that protects counters from knife marks when cutting food
parchment paper	paper used for baking that keeps food from sticking to the baking sheet
platter	large dish meant for serving food
ramekin	individual serving-size baking dish
saucepan	pan with a long handle, lid, and high sides for use on the stovetop
skillet	pan with a long handle and low sides for use on the stovetop; also called a frying pan
spatula	utensil used for mixing, spreading, or scraping the sides of pots and bowls
stockpot	large, round metal pot for use on the stovetop with handles on each side and a lid
turner	utensil with a flat end used to flip food over or remove it from a pan
whisk	tool used to break down ingredients and bring air into a mixture

Terms

al dente	cook until food is soft, but still has some firmness
brine	liquid made from water and salt used to preserve food
cream	mix foods until smooth
deglaze	add a liquid to a skillet to dissolve bits of food stuck on the bottom
dice	cut into small pieces (smaller than chopping, but bigger than mincing)
drizzle	pour a liquid lightly over food
evaporate	heat so that liquid changes to vapor
marinate	soak in a liquid and spices to add flavor
mince	cut into very fine pieces
sauté	cook in a pan with a little fat, such as oil or butter
serrated	having an uneven, jagged edge for cutting
simmer	cook over low heat so that the liquid bubbles gently, but does not boil
to taste	amount that tastes best to you
whisk	beat quickly with a whisk to break down ingredients and bring air into a mixture

Find Out More

Books

Blaxland, Wendy. *Italian Food*. Mankato, MN: Smart Apple Media, 2012.

Locricchio, Matthew. *The Cooking of Italy*. New York: Marshall Cavendish Benchmark, 2012.

Mara, Wil. *The Romans*. New York: Marshall Cavendish Benchmark, 2012.

Steele, Philip. *Hail! Ancient Romans*. New York: Crabtree, 2011.

Wagner, Lisa. *Cool Italian Cooking: Fun and Tasty Recipes for Kids*. Minneapolis: ABDO, 2011.

DVDs

Macaulay, David. *Roman City*. Alexandria, VA: PBS Home Video, 2006.

Mori, Valeria. *Countries Around the World: Italy*. Wynnewood, PA: Schlessinger Media, 2007.

Web Sites

BBC: Primary History: Romans
www.bbc.co.uk/schools/primaryhistory/romans
Explore interactive pages full of facts, photos, and videos.

KidsHealth: Being Safe in the Kitchen
http://kidshealth.org/kid/watch/house/safe_in_kitchen.
html
Read tips to keep you safe as you cook.

MyPlate
www.choosemyplate.gov
This site describes a healthy, balanced way to get all the
nutrients you need.

National Geographic Kids: Italy
kids.nationalgeographic.com/kids/places/find/italy
View videos, look at maps, and read lots of information at
this interactive site.

Time for Kids: Italy
www.timeforkids.com/destination/italy
Visit this site to see lots of pictures, learn some Italian,
and follow an Italian girl through her day.

Further Research

If this book gave you a taste for Italian food, there are
many more Italian cookbooks you could look at. You
could also locate Italian restaurants or bakeries in your
own town or city to try a bite of authentic Italian dishes.

You may also be curious about Italy's history and culture.
Stop into your local library and ask a librarian to help you
learn more. Or ask a parent to help you look up Web sites
for recipes, museums, or other information about Italy.

Index